WHIMSICAL RHAPSODY

BY

Dr. EJINE OKOROAFOR - EZEDIARO

Copyright © Dr. Ejine Okoroafor-Ezediaro 2007

All Rights reserved. No part of this book may be reproduced, stored in a retrieved system or transmitted, in any form or by any means, electronic, mechanical, photocopying, recording or otherwise, without the written prior permission of the author.

ISBN 978-0-6151-5905-8

Dedicated to my hubbilicious
Ikenna Ezediaro

*Everybody has a story
And every soul, a sonnet*

INTANGIBLES

SOULMATE

Take my palm and I hope you can feel my pulse
Look into my eyes and you will view my depth
Hug me and share the warmth of my body
Kiss me and taste the nectar of my soul
Nuzzle my neck and feel the softness of my skin
Snuggle to my chest and strum to the beat of my heart
Sing with me and sorrows are bound to flee
Dance with me and enjoy the music of love
Pray with me for realization of like dreams
Stride along with me on this walk of life
Lets stay together as soul mates for life.

HOME

My heart lies within your fold
Therein lies the sanctuary of my weary body
Your different rooms like chambers of my soul
Each reminiscent of an event or memory
I might travel to the choicest city
Yet long to be embraced back in your arms
I could lie on the silkiest sheets
But my best sleep is within your abode
In your stead, I walk around bare
With candour and fearing no judgment
Your little nooks and corners
Witness to my fantasies and secret delights
Yet I trust you to never let me down
All the pieces of my soul
Like jigsaw puzzle fall into place
Once I step across your threshold
For you are home,
Where my heart and soul belongs

LIFE

Sustained by air we breathe
Fortified by hope and faith
Watered by food we devour
Worn by abrasion of our soul

Sunned by triumphs and little mercies
Scheduled by employment or studies
Rained by disappointment or woes
Lit by the loves of our lives
Set amok by kids we beget

Sometimes overwhelming or arduous
Others, exciting from sheer discord
Each day, a suspense unfolded by night
Then sleep, not devoid of mystery
To a pregnant tomorrow
Offspring unbeknown

That's life's relentless grind of cycles
That's life – the life that we live.

CROSSROADS

Evocative of lines across one another
Middle held by a pivotal centerpiece
Opposites but parallels strung crosswise
The direction of the dangle, we decide

Love and hate are but passions apart
Faith and atheism are beliefs apart
Control or anger swayed by sheer willpower
Sanity from madness sharing an act denominator

Desire from detest devoid of passion
Happiness and sadness cloaked by attitude
Knowledge or Ignorance, opposing lines of the diagonal
Adolescence into Adulthood illustrated by maturity

Poverty and wealth but pennies removed
Life from death, just breaths demarcated
Good and evil are deeds in dispute
Day from night are hours ticked separate

Few of the vertices of our existence
At crossroads with our very subsistence
For we hold our destiny in our palm and the course
Of life is ours to decide, for we are after all
Masters of our emotions and providence

Nuptials

Evolution of friendship into kinship
Union of both mind and money
Love is the ultimate base
God and religion are requisite
Compromise is the rock layer
Tolerance carves the door
While respect is the key
Trust is mandatory
But truth is essential
Study your partner
Understand one another
Grow into each other
Aim at influencing, not exterminating
The other's personality
Allow breathing space occasionally
Adjust to individual needs
Togetherness upholds unity
Laughter and humor
Are basic ingredients
Add different flavors and spices
To replenish and rekindle bond
Deal with good and bad cards
With equal candour
Never take the other for granted
For better and/or for worse
Ultimate mantra for marriage
I am no expert
Nonetheless, here's my thought

PRIVATE RUMINATION

UNBORN

I dreamt you
I lived you
I saw you
With your father's ears and my eyes
And my nose but his mouth
With his face but my smile
His height but my figure

I couldn't wait to meet you
I patted my big belly
Felt you nestled inside
Your kick was a thrill
My boobs engorged
To enrich and feed you

I touched your face
I stroked your silky skin
They were real in my dreams
I whispered that I loved you
With all my heart and soul
But it was a dream

Will I ever get to meet you?
Will I ever see and touch you?
I tried nature and needles
I tried everything else but yet
I still believe that one day we shall meet
The beautiful stranger of my dreams
Who will make my life real?

Yen

In every child, I see your face
Every mum cradling a bundle of joy, I covet
Wishing each protruding belly was us
Yearning to complete our family

You and I
Will one day be?
I pray daily
That will come to be

I've longed for you since yesterday
I need you more everyday
I hope one day you'll know
I fell in love with you before you were

I yearn for you so much,
It hurts
I long to cradle you in my arms
Rock you to sleep
Feed you and coo at you

I've never wanted anything
Else more
Each day I pray for you
And know
Someday hopefully soon
We'll get to meet
Whether yin or yang.

Ode to my mother

You nourished the egg that formed me
Nine months in your womb I lay
Protected and shielded while I matured
Then into the world I was propelled
The link uncut even as the cord was cut
You guided and nurtured me still
Through the maze of my childhood
Guiding me the right way out of the muddle
And even in my teenage days
When I thought I held the world in my palm
You patiently listened and bore with me
You wiped my tears when I cried
You shared my joy when I excelled
You encouraged me when I was low
You stood by me when no one else would
You believed in me even when my dreams
Seemed beyond my scope
You were the rock on which I lay
And when life began to make sense
And an adult I became
With all the virtues you imbibed in me
You left like a tree felled in its prime
The fruit of your labor you never reaped
Guess heaven needed you more than I do
I love you mama and will always do
Your smile is forever encased on my soul
The memories of you is an anchor
That I will rely on for the rest of my life.

Adieu grandmother

Your departure was sorrowful
and we are mournful
your life cupped almost a century
so we are celebratory

You loved Life
a virtue we imbibe
Your knack for extravagant words
many a laughter when retold
your ingenuity
a tutorial for livelihood
your outlook was always
to live and let others live

We miss your superb dishes
and the ultimate Grandma recipes
we pine for nights spent in your abode
listening to countless tales and folklores
or basking in the liberty
As only would be bestowed
By an indulgent Grandma

Adieu Grandma
we miss you
we love you
but God loves you more.

Our Journey

Like an infant's, our steps faltered
When we started out on this journey
Tentative baby steps, they were that we took
But our confidence gradually grew
With every step, our stride became more assured
we stumbled occasionally
But rose with renewed determination

Soon we began to stand without support
our feet growing stronger and firmer
rooted in a deeper understanding of ourselves
we learnt to retrace missed steps
And endeavored to thread the right course

We treaded by, not across a rose garden
Or else the prickly thorns could have entangled us
but we enjoyed the whiff that wafted our way

We've savored thrills and weathered falls
Hopefully we will last the distance
But the cadence of this journey
And it's eventual destination
Are doors that we hold the key?

MUSE

A Teenager's elegy
(Open letter to parents)

I am trudging along this path of life
With just my wits pitted against the world
I continue to make my way through the puddle
With my feet deeply embedded in mud
As I beat my path through the shrubs
Sometimes I trip and fall but stand
Undeterred, dust myself and trudge on
Others I grope through darkness
Blindly trying to feel my way out
Hoping to make it to the safe side
While I cogitate the steps taken so far
And strategize the direction of my next move
Gradually, the routes begin to appear familiar
As life unfolds steadily before my weary sight
Every hike is a lesson, every fall a consolidation
I could let you lead me all the way
But then I would have lived your life
And will remain blind, unable to find my way if alone
So sometimes we need to severe ties
To discern the strength and weaknesses in ourselves
And make and learn from own mistakes
And at a point, you have to let love loose
And if it does not return to you
Then it never did belong to you.

Rhetoric

I stand unshackled yet feel restricted,
can't take flight without permit

My mouth is open yet voice is thin
Afraid of recrimination and condemnation
for my speech is dictated by societal norms.

My soul is free yet thoughts are restrained,
hampered by religious cum scientific conflicts.

My skin is its color and a plain coat,
yet defines me more than the inherent human in me.

My eyes are wide-open yet are blinded
By atrocities and iniquities abounding my surrounding

My ears are receptive but drummed deaf
By diatribe, senseless shootings and vicious warfare

My arms are free but feel restrained and reluctant to hug
Male or female for fear of hetero- and homo- tags.

Our world embodies like minds in hopes and aspirations
Yet is riddled with multiple divides and differences

In the wide expanse of mother earth
Extensive enough to encompass multitude nations
But is plagued by segregation and warfare

In a free world, I stand fragile and vulnerable
weighed down by a ton of bondage and restriction
What is free? Whither our world?

Dilemma

Ever been caught in a tide?
Or tried to ride against waves
While the intensity grows
And waves become tetchy
More tumultuous by the stroke
But you try to persevere
Grasping at any lifeline
While contemplating options
Hoping the shore draws near
But unwittingly relishing the wild toss
Albeit wishing for the storm to abate
As you struggle to stay afloat
Or else be swept away or sink

Sooner than later
The storm abates
Abruptly swept into a deadly calm
Eerie and spookier
Even worse than the raging storm
Whither the waves you wonder?
It has become too tranquil for comfort
May be a quieter storm or nosier calm?
You start to contemplate

That's the conflicted nature of human desire
Transitory with time and situation
And such is the varied emotions
Rotating round the orbit of human psyche
In a continual search
And quest for eventual satisfaction

WALLS

Caught up in a spot
And one of those moments
As walls closed in on me
Wherever I turn is a bump
I swirl around, step forward
Then backward but no escape

It's another hitch in
The rollercoaster of Life
I've tried to enjoy the ride
Exhilaration at intervals
Trepidation at others
And a few obvious despair

Woops of joy, cries of woe
Laughter, screams and yells
I turn around and it's still walls
Closing in and no perceptible getaway
Until I spied a tiny flicker of light

As it glimmered into hope
And I prayed to the Lord, my solace
The only one that never fails me
And I beseeched him, my savior
For speedy and immediate delivery

I was reassured as the walls started to fall
And I awaited salvation and triumph
For survival is only by his might
For if the Lord be with me
Then who could be against me?
I beseeched the Lord to stay with me.

Diabolical

Encased in a cocoon
Wrapped in sugarcoated wraps
Smelling like a rose
Until the bubble was burst
And your true colors revealed

Glib tongued not considerate
Smooth and suave but like a snake
Smart a cover-up for cowardice
Confidence was just a cloak
Playing on my vulnerabilities

Can see you clearly now
Revealed in full deceitful splendor
Smothering and pushy
Shackles off now, dear
No longer slave to your Lies

Inspirational

In honor of unsung heroes

Did anyone say what you mean to them?
Did they mention how much they appreciate you?
Did anyone ever tell you that you are a star?
Did you ever comprehend the depth of your deeds?

So we want to tell you today!
We want to say you are great
and let you know you're our rock
and one in a million

When we were low, you lifted our spirits
when we were up; you shared our joy
when we cried, you offered not only a shoulder
But helped wipe our tears
You never failed us in times of need
repeatedly you reinforced the meaning of trust
in you, we found the true meaning of friendship

We hope that we aren't just takers but givers too
because that will only belie the lessons derived

But today our friend, we want you to know
that you are a crucial part of our life.

You are our hero!

Never give up

When it feels like the world is on your shoulders
Weighing down like a ton of rocks.
And it seems like there is no respite
For your decisions offer no solace.

When doors are seemingly slammed in your face
And daily, your problems seem to compound
and it seems like your lot is the worse
As everyone else seems to be in top form

Never forget the silver lining in the sky
And that if you are patient enough, you will find it
Recall that God is watching and will break your fall
For he never forsakes his children

Be reminded that a storm invariably abates
When treacherous waves lapse into calm
Keep in mind that hot eventually cools
As does ill luck morph into good fortune

Disappointments are blessings in disguise
as easy come, so does easy go
Success by toil is more fulfilling
Than that tossed into our lap

So whenever you feel down and low,
Succor in the words of this verse.

All that matters

Life's trail is never clear cut
Stumbling blocks fill the way
Stumble and fall, you'll do
But in the end, you'll overcome
To reach endpoints
Achieve milestones
Success nonetheless, in spite of duration

Play neither a victim, nor a whiner be
Appreciate whatever comes your way
Sometimes it feels like you are being teased
So be upbeat, smile in the face of adversity

Your lot is no worse than the next man's
Stay grateful for every experience derived
Assimilate the lessons provided
Annotate but don't internalize
Feel low and wallow in self pity
Beat yourself up if you will

Then dust yourself up and soldier on
Find a mature release outlet
Don't give up
Don't worry
Set your goal
Have a dream
It is just a matter of time
With hard work, faith and luck
You will reach that summit
And that is all that matters.

Make your day

What a difference, a day makes
Yesterday was today until dawn
Today, almost yesterday by dusk

Time just flies us by
Impossible to recapture
But memories are made
As days speed past
And time winds down
Ticking across the orbit of a clock
Tick-tock from seconds
Into minutes then hours
To days, weeks, months and years

We can only reflect on the past
Regret mistakes or steps not implemented
But then we can twiddle with the future
Today is therefore the day
We make amends for yesterday
And vow to further enhance tomorrow
We may not be able to recapture time
But we can strive to better ensuing days

So if we choose, we can make today
A better day than yesterday was
And tomorrow even better
Then time is not totally lost but made

Let us make our time and day
Let us make each other's day.

ANGER

Stars implode in the eyes
Head explodes into a thousand daggers
Mouth is froth with numerous syllabuses
Mind is filled with murderous thoughts
Hands shake with emotion and feet tremble

Take a minute and step back
What was the trigger?
Minute matter!
On a different day
Might have aroused laughter

Step aside
Far from the barrel of wicked words
Distant from the furious exchange
Take a deep breath
Pull your thoughts together

Quick to anger
Quick to harm
Restraint is called for
Remorse and regret
Oft too late
To repair done damage

So step aside and back, Rethink
A dance step to learn when rage looms.

Quirky Droll

MEMOIR

Clearly just like yesterday
The memory of us is envisioned
We bonded and waltzed a love melody
relishing each other's company
As we chatted late into the night
Never loss for words and our laughter
Like a merry chime, rang across the hall way

Subtle changes soon reared their head
Evident signs that I chose to disregard
hoping they will simultaneously disappear
But naïve I was, refusing to read the signs
For what they were, the novelty had worn off for you

reminiscent of a scene off the discovery channel
of a lion after a prey for dinner, scheming, prancing
Running and even a strut
Wholly absorbed in the object of its intent
Prey finally caught after the rigmarole
He proceeded to devour the good parts
carcass soon discarded and tussled away
Even more swiftly than the chase
the attraction weaned after its purpose was served
and off went the beast for another prey to catch

Same as the male after a female quarry
all loving till evil bid accomplished
Then swagger off to find another damsel prey.

Is that the audacity of the male or the order of creation?
For males to disrupt the female lives and walk away
No explanation tendered.
With the poor female left forlorn
Like a carcass with its best part gone
wondering why and when it all went wrong.

Straphangers

Hello, I dared to mutter
Hello, the reluctant answer
Opposite me sat another
Bent on averting my glance
While I pretend not to notice
In the midst of an indifferent audience

A fellow lackadaisically sat across two seats
The frail old lady adjacent clutching handbag to chest
Or the little ones tugging at their mother for comfort
Lady afar, dressed to the nines and city workers in suit
Lads in trousers beneath their waist, unsecured with belt
Showing off briefs and pants, "just fashion" they assert

The school kids at the end of the carriage
Chattering at the top of their voice
Bent on forcing strangers into their repartee
Amidst the drone of muted dialogue
In English and diverse tongue
Or the hustler, slyly hawking his cargo
While negotiating through the standing throng

A constellation of Homo sapiens
And cross-section of people, colors and races
Diverse in both origin and cultures

Where y' all are headed?
Work, retail therapy or home
Maybe tourists on a thrill quest
Or few on a clandestine summit
All engrossed in stops or stations

A prevailing pungent smell of sweat pervaded
Blended with an assortment of perfumes
In the cramped space while citizens and aliens jostled

An eclectic mix of walks of life
A silent interaction of ranks
No evident distinction whatsoever
In the confinement of that little space

Klickity Klink went the train
As we shared the ride

We were strangers but straphangers
At our respective stop, we disappear
Back to our individual worlds

Rain coat

While caught up in the rain
Pelted by the furious water jets
And drenched to my skin
Soaked and dribbling wet
Before the tears began to pour
Mingling with the rain water
I barely tasted the saltiness of teardrops
Trickling down from cheeks into lips
Since neutralized by the rain water
I wore no coat but the rain was my cover
Under its cloak, I bashed my soul out
All pent up frustration released
As the rain pounced
Cleansing both soul and body
My anguish mirrored as dismay
To an unsuspecting onlooker
At the audacity of the unannounced downpour
The water pellets thumped furiously
In tune with my anguished blubbery
I ran against the wind on the footpath
Albeit to liberate my anguish
Than to escape the furious shower
My laden sorrow ebbing in the face
Of the uplifting wind
Tears and raindrops washed away gloom
As both heaven and I washed out our grime

An allusion to lost childhood when we had played in the rain
But those were days of innocent fun and fond memories
Not of concealed sorrow revamped in the rain
Such is innocence tarnished even in the purity of the rain

Be warned!

He's playing out his insecurities
While trying to lay it on you
Putting you down and
Calling you names
Or prodding at you

He should get it by now
He isn't taking you down
You'll not be reduced to his level
Nor will he break your spirit

Be comfortable in your skin
And let nobody define you
Your mama brought you up
And molded you, ingraining self worth
And endless worthy possibilities

So let no bully tell you otherwise
Hold your head up any where or time
You owe no one explanations
So demand none from no one

If he gets himself into frenzy
Twisted in his rage pants
And try to humiliate you
He'd better think again
Because he is only manifesting
His vulnerability and insecurity

Patriotism

UHAMIRI-THE BLUE LAKE

The Lady of all Lakes
Clad in bluish-green splendour
Shimmering within its grand shore
Underneath houses the mermaids
Ogbuide, the quintessence of them all

A semi-peninsula for the town Ameshi
Natural boundary demarcating neighbours

On your course, you tease Urashi
The confluence of your reverberating sapphire
And the rusty tan of Urashi
Where your water swiftly retreats to itself
Refusing to be contaminated
By the harsh brown river
A majestic sight and freak of nature
Fit to rank amongst wonders of the world

You bask in the glory of your assets
Sating tastes and fish feeding mouths
Your tide overflows with rain
Receding into a sandy beach for Harmattan

Therein lies your ageless radiance
A proud sight for your people
From the merry and delightful land
The flamboyant people of Ameshi

Resilience of Mother Nation

Weep not my child, but save your tears
For the honorably departed
Who in combat restored glory to this soil
And toiled for betterment of the community
Don't waste tears on this calamity
Senseless blood shed or
Brothers turned against their brethren
Because of greed, self loathing and iniquity

Wipe your tears my child and take my hand
While I lean on you for my body is afflicted
My spirit is broken and my soul is lost
Afflicted and rattled like a doll
No cure foreseen but solace in faith and future

Smile instead my child and nurture thy hope
Of restoring the glory of the giant that once was
Of recovering lost resources in foreign accounts
And hopes of taps that run and electricity that stay alight
Of roads that are pliable and houses that never leak

For that day, when your sorrow reverts to laughter
Then my broken body will be whole again
When from my eventually lactating breast, you will feed again
When from my revived and fertile soil, you will harvest
If only all my children hearkens to the voice of reason

I wish you peace my child and bid you no more tears
Conserve your energy for the tasks ahead
Gather your wits to tackle the obstacles
The arduous task that will nurse me back to health
For my fate hinges on the conscience of my progeny

Down memory lane

Remember the days of yore
When we marched, waving the flag
Green, white and green fluttering in the air
We deemed the sky our limit
We were future leaders of tomorrow
We were the giant of Africa
The oil boomed our immense wealth
Intensifying and typifying our hopes for a better tomorrow

Forty and more years later
We have marched two steps forward
And regressed five steps backward
Unlike wine, we failed to mature with age
Or learnt from our mistakes
Failing to adopt measures for the betterment
And progress of our once young nation

But what became of us as a nation?
What became of as a people?

A massive exodus of the populace
To lands afar in search of greener pastures
Or in frustrated defiance and away from
A land where leaders siphon millions while thousands starve
Yet sleep through the night undeterred by conscience
While kids starve and education is shoddy
Where few of the youth are decadence prone
Resorting to scams in the name of smart
Where reputation both home and abroad
Has sunk beneath reprehensible
As the rich get richer daily while the poor get poorer
For while the monkey toils, only the baboon chops

We once proclaimed our heritage with pride
But now almost scurry with head hung in shame
For fear of judgment and recrimination
The bad apples have completely spoilt the good
Whither our future?
Whither lays our fate?
When and how shall we mend?

The center and the grassroots are fallen apart
Shattered into pieces like a broken china cup

Who will pick the pieces?
Which generation shall mend us?

We are beating a hollow drum
And dancing the music of the dead
We mourn a live nation and
State lost in the wilderness
We ignored the sense of reason
That had shone like floodlight
And only the blind could have missed

We are a nation failed by its leaders
And culpable by our deeds
We chose to be blind when we could see
And deaf when we could hear
Until irreparable damages were done

We still have a chance at greatness
And resources to mend fences
We have the fortitude and resilience for a comeback
If only responsibility is adopted by every single one
Morality taught to plebs and priorities put in place

We can still be the Nigeria, the nation that we once hailed

MALARIA

Just like mud lying in wait
Post torrential downpour
Waiting for whom to trip
You wait, lurking at corners
Your mosquito harbingers hovering
With proboscis ready to pierce
And inject a venomous malaria dose

This time, I'm determined to evade you
Sunday, Sunday prophylaxis
Insecticides sprayed
Nap underneath a net
Ha, see if you can catch me now
For once, I refuse to fall victim

Yet I rouse, weary to the bone
Worse than the farmer
Returning home after an
Overnight toil at Enuigbo Abatu

Head feels heavier than a ton of lead
Body hotter than coal,
a bowl of soup could warm on my forehead
Yet I shiver, shaking like Igbokoro masquerade
Dancing to the beat of akanka drums
Hallucinating and gibbering
More eloquent than Ojugo
Entranced and haunted by the spirits

You win, bloodshot eyes plead for mercy
Bitter quinines contrive a cure
I surrender and fall into deep slumber to await verdict

Nostalgia

When Harmattan and fog set in
We were undeterred and carefree
For yuletide was imminent

Entailing repeated trips to the tailor
For measurements and fittings
Even the house got a make over
An acrid smell of paint permeated
Then new curtains and decorations
Presents and gifts wrapped in readiness
All heightening the air of festivity

Christmas finally arrives
Dressed in colorful new garments
And elders in their Sunday best
We troop to church
Filled to the brim in commemoration
The sermon's protracted
The chorus heartier
The hymns are merrier
Everyone seems to belt out hymns
With an added vigor

Afterwards, we head back home
A bountiful dinner waits
Luscious bowls of jollof rice
Hefty chunks of chicken
Salad thrown in for a treat
Kids arrive in numbers
To share our banquet and hope for extra change

All in all, those were the best days

AMORE

LOVE QUEST

I seek love that is pure
I crave love that is reciprocal
Love that is unsullied and true
Until then, I remain a victim of my dreams

I seek passionate love
Love that propels the heart with sheer joy
Flutters the body in ecstasy, at a mere touch
Or melts the soul, at the sound of a voice

I seek love that is real
That wrought neither a dreamer nor victim
Love with links extending ways beyond
And after the waft of its freshness rescind

That is the love I seek
The love that overcomes
Is unpretentious and genuine
Forgiving and abiding
Caring and giving
That's love that I seek

Cupid

I settle for sleep
Wrapped cozily beneath sheets
Hoping he will call
My heart is despondent
My soul goes a wandering
Conjuring images of prince charming
Because Cupid is coming my way

He will convey a bowl of roses
And bring me love
Love is Roses
Roses are for love
Cupid with the bow
The man after my heart
Shoot the arrow through my soul
For love that will lighten my heart

As for my prince
His soul will be pierced deeper
And our hearts shall merge into one
Melt and reemerge entwined
And we'll waltz along to the tune
Of sweet love music strung by Cupid

Don't let love drag you down

Love is not going to drag you down
If you don't let it
Don't sit and stare as the days pass you by
while you skulk in the shadows
Snooping or eavesdropping for footsteps
eagerly awaiting the knock that never comes
Imagining every sound will bring him home
but don't let "love" drag you down

Stop tormenting yourself or remain gloomy
Neither be amazed at the perils of unreciprocated love
nor be bemused at the depth of wasted emotions wrought
Stop pitying or bashing the irony of unrequited love
because love is not trying to drag you down

No, it isn't going to bring you down
Have your cry and weep, mourn your loss
But only for a short period
If it's over, it's over

Then dust your self up
If he doesn't want you
He probably doesn't deserve you
Stop lamenting
at the injustice or folly of emotions

Just get you off that couch
Get a make over and party
Go out and grab it
For love is out there and up for grabs
The Love you deserve and are deserving of you.

Like I want you to

Cloak me in your warmth and hold me
Like your life depended on it
Whisper sweet little nothings into my ears and tell me
You've never known any like me
Cradle me to your chest and hug me tightly
Like you never want to let go
Kiss me softly, sweetly and savour my taste
Like your thirst's never been fed more gratifyingly

Handle me like a delicate porcelain glass
That will break into pieces if you let go
Cherish me like you would a precious gem
That would rust and loose its worth
If it's not handled properly
Adore me like you would a child
Precious and fragile at the same time

Love and treat me right
Accept me for who I am
Understand and respect me
Trust me because I love you
Like I want you to love me

Missing you

When you are away, you take a piece of me
While I hang limbless hankering for your return
Waiting to hear your voice or feel your touch
And when you lay your hand across my chest
The little pieces suddenly fall right back into place

When you are away, the world comes to a standstill
Halted by the void created by your absence
While I hang in limbo, hankering for your presence
And when our lips meet again
I'm suddenly given a new lease back to life

When you are away, the birds chime a sad song
The sun loses it shine and the rain pours with sorrow
While I hang in the deluge, wishing you were with me
For when you are around
The world is suddenly a much better place to live

When you are away, the sun goes with you
The night is grim without you by my side
I lay my head on the indentation of yours on the pillow
And catch a whiff of your lingering perfume
Until I reach out to embrace you and grasp thin air
That's when reality of your absence hits me

When you are away, I miss you
So sorely it hurts much worse than a boil
Being away from you is never easy
For you are a part of me, one that completes me
Being apart is sometimes necessitated
But I always miss you so much

Why?

There you go again
Collapsing the bridge we built
Lashing out with your venomous words
As you spew and foam in the mouth
Succeeding in breaking all the blocks
Destroying our mended bridge again

There you go again
Annihilating the lull
When I had just began
To appreciate our love
And revel in why I had fallen in love
With you in the first place
But you have to go and spoil it all

Why do you make it hard for me to stay in love with you?

Somber reflections

Identity Crisis

He was born in a land
Where his father acquired a passport
But insists his origins are elsewhere
Reiterating he hails from his motherland
From the tropics where the sun sets yearlong
And torrential rains and thunder zigzags
To depict the ire of the gods

He barely feels any affinity to that land
That his father insists is his own
Or to his endless tales of the homeland
Once enthralling but now confusing

He couldn't identify with either his father's land or pride
Nor his endless incantation of the glory of his land
Where he'd basked at dawn or dusk
Munching corn on the cob, roasted in open fire
Eaten with luscious peculiar ube pear
Or the fresh tilapia fish still swimming around
In the fish sellers basin when bought
To be slaughtered later and made into nsala soup
Which they enjoyed with relish
Combined with warm pounded yam fufu
Fresh from the mortar
Or the days when they trooped to the town center
To watch the masquerades, swaying to the ominous drums
Its followers with chalk marks encircling their raccoon eyes
Swapping the palm fronds to make way across the crowd
The uninitiated fleeing the path to avoid a curse

His father was nostalgic for the nights
When as kids, they'd assemble in their compound

While the elders regaled them with folklores and tales
And they chanted endless songs or solved riddles
Late into the night, retiring just before the cock crowed
To announce the crack of dawn
But that was his father's reality not his.
He stood befuddled and wondered
Where his loyalty lay
To the foreign land his father calls his own?
Or this culture he is born into
Which his father berates as foreign?

He was caught right in the middle
Born and bred in the USA
How then is his reality Africa?
How can he feel kinship to the land he barely knows?
How can he proclaim a nation that is foreign to him as his own?

Even the tales that his father narrated
Could only be a figment of his imagination
For when he arrived to reclaim his root
The sun was too harsh and none could bask
The roads were deplorable
Electricity in short supply and water scarce
He tried to conform but it was hard
He respected his father's undying loyalty
And immense pride for this lost land

However where does he stand?

He was caught in the middle
Unsure of which was his reality or identity.

His Father's Story

He had traveled across seas
Been bundled across borders
Hid and cradled in a car boot
Until he got to the Promised Land
Where he'd arrived to
Seek greener pastures

He toiled and scrapped
Remunerations sent home
For his brethren left behind
And strove for a better tomorrow
For his begotten offspring

He missed his homeland
The spirit of kinship
The camaraderie and sense of community
He was not just a statistics there
But a force to be reckoned with
He had roots
Spread far and wide
Like the deep-rooted iroko tree
Planted at the centre of his kindred home

He missed and hankered for his youth
For the carefree days when they basked in the sun
Ate and roamed freely in the town
Dancing with the masquerade
Or intermingling with his age grade
Ribbing, challenging and jollying
To return home later to his mother's food
Or retired to a friend's home

He looked around him
And it was a new world
Fast evolving before his very eyes
He would have thought things will change
But for the better
He was unimpressed by the audacity
Of the modern kids
Retorting and remonstrating their parents
He balked at the sight
Of parents restricted from disciplining their kids
Sparing the rod and spoiling the kids
He could not stomach the violence on TV
Nor the copycat kids totting guns
And the endless senseless shootings

He vowed he'd imbibe similar virtues
Same as his father before him
This culture was strange and not his
They were just passing through

Their roots and origins
Lay in his motherland
Where children knew their place
And parents are held in reverence
Where the sense of community prevailed
And each was his brother's keeper

Nay, this sure is a foreign land
Culture's too decadent for his gentle soul
He insists therefore
That his son originated
From his motherland

Tirade

I am black and proud
Hail from Ogutahood
Descendant of the homeland
Africa the motherland

Job equipped and candid
Ready and up for challenge
Believe in equal opportunities
Never going to play the race card

That was a laugh
Because nothing defines one
More than their skin
Enter an upscale shop
Eyes track your every move

Stopped a zillion times
Verification of particulars
To ascertain eligibility
Gone to the bank once
White lady dropped her purse
Comes back, glares at me
Like I had snatched it away from her
Still never going to play that card

Go house hunting
Sisters sitting outside braiding hair
Bros shirtless and hanging out at the porch
Nay, not a good neighborhood
I have worked too hard
I'm not a sell out
But I deserve better

Go for a condominium
Fit all requirements
Until the board reviews my name
Nay, you don't fit in our neighborhood
Finally found a home
Middleclass suburbia
My neighbor takes it upon herself
To set me right
The driveway must be cleared
The doorway painted
Lawn mowed
Or else what?

Lady, I think
This is my home
I pay the mortgage
Why you wanna tell me what to do?
Nay, I never said that
Thanks, I muttered
And wondered if she goes across
To tell the others
How to live in their homes

It's not about race
I console myself
It's to maintain the prestige
And class of this 'hood

Soon she strides along
Enquires about my occupation
Just being neighborly, she said
Nosy more like, I think
Doctor, I said
Aha, her daughter is in med school too

Next day though
She refers to me as a nurse
Lady, I draw the line
I refuse to play that card
But I am not going to let no one shit on me!

Finale

Bare

I am a warrior of sorts
My sword is my pen
My prose, my shield
My inspirations, experiences
Reemerged in verses

I leave myself bare
Shot with stars
Reassessed with gavels
Ranked by a culmination
Of stars and gavels

Yet I never give up
Each day a battlefield
I charge my imagination
With new knowledge acquired
Better prose to write

Angered not by one stars
Boosted by five stars
Glad of new friends
Strangers peeping at my soul
Yet common goals bind.

Author's Profile

EJINE OKOROAFOR-EZEDIARO is the author of acclaimed 'A Rose in Bloom', a contemporary African tale narrating the coming of age of a young Nigerian girl, Nkiru.

The tale chronicles the dichotomy between modernity and tradition and is available on http//www.trafford.com/06-1468 , Amazon and various other sites on the internet as well as directly from the author.

Ejine is also a practicing medical doctor and hails originally from Oguta, Nigeria. She attended Girls High School, Oguta and University of Port Harcourt where she obtained a B.Sc. in Physics before studying medicine in Ukraine.

She presently resides in NY, USA after relocating to join her spouse from the United Kingdom.

Ejine has always exhibited a flair for writing prose and poetry from childhood but only pursued this gift diligently while sitting for the United States Medical Licensing Exams.

Some of her poems are published in the Anthologies; 'Twilight Musings', 'Songs of Honor' as well as other sites on the internet.

She is presently working on the sequel to 'The Rose in Bloom' as well as other books.

Acknowledgement

I'll use this opportunity to express my gratitude to a few of my dearest ones.

I invariably thank God for all mercies and possibilities.

My sincere gratitude and love to my other half, Ikenna Ezediaro. Hubby, this one is for you.

My salute goes to my dearest father, Mr. Akaraka Okoroafor. I love you papa.

My beloved sister, Agboma Okoroafor, delightful to the eye and mind, I adore you Big Sis.

To Ogbuagu and Ogbuefi Newton Okaru, my surrogate parents, I say thank you for everything and more.

Special mention and regards to my "brothers" Ifeanyi Okoroafor and Ikenna Okoroafor.

And Felicitations to Aunty Rose Ibuaka, Aunty Pat. Nzeribe, Okonya Okoroafor, Norah Nzeribe, Ikechukwu Okoroafor, Anthony Animba, Eze Ugwueze, Dammo Audid, Mimi Achebe, Manny Ezediaro and many others.

Preface

Whimsical Rhapsody is a collection of free style poems. I have utilized a peculiar humour and wittiness in their composition.

They culminate from past and present events. Their inspirations derive from personal and public experiences, as well as general world events.

I hope you can find one to identify, empathize or laugh with but my most important desire however is to be inspirational.

www.ingramcontent.com/pod-product-compliance
Lightning Source LLC
Chambersburg PA
CBHW020022050426
42450CB00005B/607